Grenada

Everything You Need to Know

Introduction to Grenada 6

A Brief History: From Indigenous Peoples to Colonial Rule 9

Grenada's Independence: A Triumph of Sovereignty 12

The Geography of Grenada: Spice Isle Wonders 15

Climate and Weather: Tropical Paradise All Year Round 18

Flora and Fauna: Exploring Grenada's Natural Riches 20

Cuisine of Grenada: Spice Up Your Palate 22

Nutmeg and Beyond: The Spice Trade Legacy 24

Exploring Grenada's Beaches: Sun, Sand, and Serenity 27

Underwater Wonders: Diving and Snorkeling Hotspots 29

Waterfalls and Hiking Trails: Discovering Grenada's Interior 32

Grenada's National Parks: Preserving Natural Treasures 34

Carriacou: A Gem within a Gem 36

Petite Martinique: The Quintessential Caribbean Escape 38

St. George's: A Historic and Picturesque Capital 41

History Comes Alive: Forts and Museums of Grenada 43

Grenadian Festivals: Celebrating Culture and Tradition 45

Music and Dance: Vibrant Rhythms of the Spice Isle 47

The Artistic Heritage of Grenada: Craftsmanship and Creativity 50

Religion and Spirituality: Diverse Beliefs in Harmony 53

Language and Linguistic Heritage: The Melody of Creole 56

Education in Grenada: Nurturing Minds for the Future 58

Economy and Industry: Beyond the Nutmeg Trade 61

Government and Politics: Democratic Principles in Action 64

Healthcare and Wellness: Holistic Approaches to Well-being 67

Transportation in Grenada: Navigating the Island's Terrain 70

Hospitality and Accommodation: Where to Stay and What to Expect 73

Shopping in Grenada: Souvenirs and Local Crafts 75

Agriculture and Farming: Beyond Nutmeg and Cocoa 78

Sustainable Tourism Initiatives: Preserving Paradise for Generations 81

Grenada's Role in the Caribbean Community: Cooperation and Collaboration 84

Grenada's Influence on the World Stage: Diplomacy and Global Relations 87

Grenada's Literary Heritage: Words that Reflect the Soul 90

Sports and Recreation: Thrills on Land and Sea 92

Exploring Grenada's Nightlife: From Calypso to Rum Punch 95

Grenada's Healthcare System: Providing Care for All 98

Disaster Preparedness and Resilience: Weathering the Storms 101

Social Issues and Challenges: Building a Stronger Community 103

Volunteerism and Philanthropy: Giving Back to Grenada 106

Exploring Grenada's Neighborhood: Relations with Nearby Islands 109

Grenada's Future: Opportunities and Challenges Ahead 112

Epilogue 116

Introduction to Grenada

Welcome to Grenada, the enchanting Jewel of the Caribbean. Nestled in the southern Caribbean Sea, Grenada is a captivating island nation renowned for its stunning natural beauty, vibrant culture, and rich history.

With a population of approximately 112,000 inhabitants, Grenada is comprised of the main island of Grenada itself, along with the smaller islands of Carriacou and Petite Martinique. Each of these islands offers its own unique charm and allure, making Grenada a diverse and multifaceted destination for travelers from around the globe.

Grenada's history is a tapestry woven with the threads of indigenous cultures, European colonization, and struggles for independence. Originally inhabited by the indigenous Arawak and Carib peoples, Grenada was first sighted by Europeans in 1498 when Christopher Columbus landed on its shores during his third voyage to the Americas. Over the centuries that followed, the island was colonized by the French and later the British, whose influences are still evident in Grenada's language, cuisine, and architecture.

In 1974, Grenada achieved independence from British colonial rule, marking a pivotal moment in its history and setting the stage for the development of a proud and sovereign nation. Since then, Grenada has emerged as a beacon of democracy and stability in the Caribbean region, with a government characterized by its commitment to democratic principles and the rule of law.

Grenada's geography is as diverse as its history, with lush rainforests, cascading waterfalls, and pristine beaches stretching along its coastline. The island's interior is dominated by towering mountains, including Mount St. Catherine, the highest peak in Grenada, which offers breathtaking views of the surrounding landscape.

The climate in Grenada is tropical, characterized by warm temperatures year-round and a refreshing trade wind breeze that provides relief from the heat. The island experiences two main seasons: the dry season, which runs from January to May, and the rainy season, which occurs from June to December. Despite occasional rainfall, Grenada's climate is generally sunny and pleasant, making it an ideal destination for outdoor activities and beach vacations.

Grenada's economy is driven by agriculture, tourism, and services, with a particular emphasis on the production of spices such as nutmeg, cinnamon, and cloves. Known as the "Spice Isle," Grenada is renowned for its aromatic spices, which are exported to markets around the world and contribute significantly to the island's economy.

In addition to its natural beauty and economic vitality, Grenada is also celebrated for its vibrant culture, which reflects the diverse influences of its indigenous, African, European, and East Indian heritage. From the pulsating rhythms of Calypso and Soca music to the colorful costumes of traditional Carnival celebrations, Grenada's cultural scene is a feast for the senses, offering visitors a rich tapestry of music, dance, and art.

In the pages that follow, we will delve deeper into the wonders of Grenada, exploring its history, geography, culture, and more. Join us on a journey of discovery as we uncover the secrets of this captivating Caribbean gem.

A Brief History: From Indigenous Peoples to Colonial Rule

The history of Grenada is a fascinating journey through time, spanning thousands of years and encompassing the rich tapestry of cultures and civilizations that have shaped the island's identity. From its earliest inhabitants to the era of European colonization, Grenada's history is marked by triumphs and challenges, conquests and resistance.

The story of Grenada begins with its indigenous peoples, the Arawak and Carib tribes, who first settled the island around 1000 AD. These resilient peoples lived in harmony with nature, cultivating crops such as cassava, sweet potatoes, and yams, and engaging in fishing and hunting to sustain their communities. The Arawak were the first to inhabit Grenada, followed by the Caribs, who arrived later and eventually became the dominant indigenous group on the island.

In 1498, Grenada was sighted by European explorers during Christopher Columbus's third voyage to the Americas. However, it wasn't until the early 17th century that European colonization of the island began in earnest. In 1609, the French established the first permanent European settlement on Grenada, laying the foundations for centuries of French influence on the island's culture, language, and society.

Over the next century, Grenada became a prized possession in the power struggles between European colonial powers, particularly France and Britain. The island changed hands several times during this period, with control alternating between the French and the British as they vied for dominance in the Caribbean region.

In 1763, Grenada was officially ceded to Britain under the terms of the Treaty of Paris, marking the beginning of a new chapter in the island's history as a British colony. Under British rule, Grenada experienced significant economic growth and development, fueled in part by the expansion of the sugar industry and the use of enslaved labor from Africa.

The 18th and 19th centuries saw Grenada prosper as a major producer of sugar and other agricultural commodities, thanks to its fertile soil and favorable climate. However, this prosperity came at a great human cost, as enslaved Africans endured harsh working conditions and brutal treatment on the island's plantations.

In 1833, slavery was abolished throughout the British Empire, leading to significant social and economic changes in Grenada and other

Caribbean colonies. The end of slavery brought new challenges and opportunities for the island's inhabitants, as former slaves sought to build lives of freedom and independence in the wake of centuries of oppression.

In 1974, Grenada achieved independence from British colonial rule, marking a historic moment of triumph for the island's people and paving the way for the development of a proud and sovereign nation. Since then, Grenada has emerged as a beacon of democracy and stability in the Caribbean region, with a government characterized by its commitment to democratic principles and the rule of law.

Today, Grenada continues to thrive as a vibrant and diverse society, with a rich cultural heritage that reflects the contributions of its indigenous, African, European, and East Indian peoples. From its ancient roots to its modern-day achievements, the history of Grenada is a testament to the resilience, spirit, and determination of its people.

Grenada's Independence: A Triumph of Sovereignty

Grenada's journey to independence is a story of courage, resilience, and the unwavering determination of its people to chart their own destiny. After centuries of colonial rule under various European powers, Grenada emerged as a sovereign nation on February 7, 1974, marking a significant milestone in its history.

The road to independence was not easy, and it was paved with struggles and sacrifices. For decades, Grenadians had agitated for greater autonomy and self-governance, seeking to break free from the shackles of colonialism and assert their right to determine their own future. This desire for independence was fueled by a growing sense of national identity and pride, as well as a recognition of the injustices and inequalities perpetuated by colonial rule.

The push for independence gained momentum in the mid-20th century, as nationalist movements emerged across the Caribbean region, advocating for political self-determination and sovereignty. In Grenada, the call for independence was led by visionary leaders such as Eric Gairy, who founded the Grenada United Labour Party (GULP) and championed the cause of national liberation.

In 1967, Grenada took a significant step towards independence with the introduction of a new constitution, which granted the island greater autonomy and paved the way for the eventual transition to full sovereignty. However, it would be several more years before Grenada would achieve independence from British colonial rule.

The path to independence was not without its challenges and setbacks. Political divisions and tensions within Grenada's society often threatened to derail the independence movement, as different factions vied for power and influence. However, despite these internal struggles, the people of Grenada remained united in their determination to break free from colonial oppression and assert their right to self-determination.

Finally, on February 7, 1974, Grenada officially achieved independence from British colonial rule, marking a historic moment of triumph for the island's people and a symbol of hope for oppressed peoples around the world. The newly independent nation was greeted with jubilation and celebration, as Grenadians rejoiced in their newfound freedom and sovereignty.

In the years that followed, Grenada embarked on a journey of nation-building and development, as it sought to establish itself as a prosperous and democratic nation in the Caribbean region. Despite facing numerous challenges along the way, including political instability and economic uncertainty, Grenada remained steadfast in its commitment to the principles of democracy, freedom, and equality.

Today, Grenada stands as a proud and sovereign nation, a shining example of what can be achieved when a people are united in their pursuit of liberty and justice. The legacy of independence continues to inspire future generations of Grenadians, as they work to build a brighter and more prosperous future for themselves and their country.

The Geography of Grenada: Spice Isle Wonders

Grenada's geography is as diverse as it is captivating, offering visitors a rich tapestry of landscapes, from lush rainforests to pristine beaches and towering mountains. Located in the southern Caribbean Sea, Grenada is part of the Lesser Antilles chain of islands, situated between the Caribbean Sea to the west and the Atlantic Ocean to the east.

The main island of Grenada is relatively small, measuring just 344 square kilometers (133 square miles) in area, yet it packs a remarkable variety of natural wonders into its compact size. The island is characterized by its rugged terrain, with volcanic peaks rising sharply from the sea and plunging valleys carpeted in dense tropical vegetation.

The centerpiece of Grenada's geography is its mountainous interior, dominated by a series of volcanic peaks that form the backbone of the island. The highest of these peaks is Mount St. Catherine, which towers 840 meters (2,760 feet) above sea level and offers breathtaking views of the surrounding landscape. Other notable peaks include Mount Qua Qua and Mount Sinai, each offering its own unique hiking experiences and opportunities for exploration.

In addition to its mountains, Grenada is also home to a number of lush rainforests and tropical jungles, which cover much of the island's interior. These dense forests are teeming with biodiversity, supporting a rich array of plant and animal species, including exotic birds, monkeys, and colorful butterflies. Grenada's rainforests are a paradise for nature lovers and outdoor enthusiasts, offering countless opportunities for hiking, birdwatching, and wildlife spotting.

Surrounding the island's interior are miles of pristine coastline, dotted with secluded coves, sandy beaches, and crystal-clear waters. Grenada boasts more than 45 beaches, each with its own unique character and charm, ranging from bustling resort areas to remote and secluded stretches of sand. Grand Anse Beach, located just south of the capital city of St. George's, is one of the most popular and picturesque beaches on the island, known for its soft white sand and calm turquoise waters.

Off the coast of Grenada lie several smaller islands and islets, including Carriacou and Petite Martinique, each offering their own distinct geography and attractions. Carriacou, the largest of Grenada's sister islands, is known for its tranquil beaches, colorful coral reefs, and vibrant cultural scene. Petite Martinique, meanwhile, is a tiny yet charming island with a laid-back atmosphere and stunning views of the surrounding sea.

In summary, Grenada's geography is a testament to the island's natural beauty and diversity, with its rugged mountains, lush rainforests, and pristine beaches combining to create a truly enchanting destination for travelers from around the world. Whether exploring the peaks of its interior, lounging on its sandy shores, or diving beneath its azure waters, visitors to Grenada are sure to be captivated by the wonders of the Spice Isle.

Climate and Weather: Tropical Paradise All Year Round

Grenada's climate is one of its most alluring attributes, drawing visitors from around the world with its promise of warm temperatures, sunny skies, and gentle trade winds. Situated in the tropics, Grenada enjoys a consistently pleasant climate year-round, making it an ideal destination for travelers seeking to escape the cold and bask in the warmth of the Caribbean sun.

The climate of Grenada is classified as tropical, characterized by high temperatures and humidity levels tempered by refreshing sea breezes. The island experiences two main seasons: the dry season, which runs from January to May, and the rainy season, which occurs from June to December. During the dry season, visitors can expect clear skies, abundant sunshine, and minimal rainfall, making it the perfect time to explore Grenada's outdoor attractions and enjoy activities such as hiking, snorkeling, and sunbathing on the beach.

In contrast, the rainy season brings higher levels of precipitation to Grenada, with brief but intense showers occurring sporadically throughout the day. Despite the occasional rain, Grenada's climate remains warm and tropical year-round, with temperatures typically ranging from 75°F to 85°F (24°C to 29°C). The island's location near the equator ensures relatively stable temperatures throughout the year, with only slight variations between seasons.

One of the most notable features of Grenada's climate is its trade winds, which blow steadily from the northeast for much of the year, providing a refreshing breeze that helps to moderate temperatures and keep humidity levels in check. These trade winds are especially welcome during the hotter months of the year, providing relief from the heat and making outdoor activities more enjoyable.

Grenada is also fortunate to lie outside the primary hurricane belt, meaning that it is less prone to direct hits from hurricanes and tropical storms compared to other islands in the Caribbean. While Grenada may occasionally experience the effects of passing storms, the island's rugged terrain and natural barriers help to mitigate the impact of severe weather events, ensuring that it remains a relatively safe and stable destination for travelers.

In summary, Grenada's climate is a key factor in its appeal as a tropical paradise, offering visitors the opportunity to enjoy warm temperatures, sunny skies, and gentle breezes throughout the year. Whether basking on the beach, exploring the rainforest, or sampling local cuisine, visitors to Grenada can look forward to a truly delightful experience in this idyllic island paradise.

Flora and Fauna: Exploring Grenada's Natural Riches

Grenada's natural riches extend far beyond its stunning beaches and lush rainforests, encompassing a diverse array of flora and fauna that call the island home. From colorful tropical flowers to rare bird species, Grenada's biodiversity is a testament to its pristine natural environment and rich ecological heritage.

The island's rainforests are teeming with life, harboring an incredible variety of plant species, many of which are found nowhere else on Earth. Towering mahogany trees, fragrant nutmeg trees, and towering palms are just a few examples of the diverse flora that flourish in Grenada's fertile soil. These forests are also home to a wealth of medicinal plants and herbs, which have been used for centuries by indigenous peoples and traditional healers for their healing properties. In addition to its lush vegetation, Grenada is also home to a rich diversity of wildlife, including numerous species of birds, mammals, reptiles, and amphibians. The island's avifauna is particularly impressive, with over 170 species of birds recorded, including colorful parrots, hummingbirds, and the rare Grenada dove, which is found only on the island. Birdwatchers flock to Grenada to catch a glimpse of these elusive species in their natural habitat, making it a popular destination for eco-tourism and birdwatching enthusiasts. Grenada's coastal waters are equally rich in biodiversity, with vibrant coral reefs, seagrass beds, and mangrove forests providing crucial habitat for a wide variety of marine life. These ecosystems support a diverse array of fish species, including colorful reef fish, sharks, rays, and sea turtles, which can be observed while snorkeling, diving, or taking a glass-bottom boat tour. Grenada is also home to several marine protected areas, which help to conserve and protect its valuable marine resources for future generations. One of the most iconic symbols of Grenada's natural heritage is its spices, which have been cultivated on the island for centuries and are celebrated for their aromatic flavors and medicinal properties. Nutmeg, cloves, cinnamon, and ginger are just a few of the spices that thrive in Grenada's fertile soil, earning the island the nickname "Spice Isle" and making it a must-visit destination for culinary enthusiasts and food lovers.

Grenada's commitment to conservation and sustainable development has helped to preserve its natural riches for future generations, ensuring that visitors can continue to explore and enjoy the island's stunning landscapes and diverse ecosystems for years to come. Whether hiking through its rainforests, snorkeling on its coral reefs, or simply relaxing on its sandy beaches, Grenada offers a wealth of opportunities for nature lovers to connect with the natural world and experience the beauty of the Caribbean in all its glory.

Cuisine of Grenada: Spice Up Your Palate

Grenadian cuisine is a delightful fusion of flavors, influenced by the island's rich cultural heritage and abundant natural resources. At the heart of Grenadian cooking lies the island's world-renowned spices, which infuse dishes with an aromatic blend of flavors and aromas that tantalize the taste buds and leave a lasting impression.

Nutmeg, cloves, cinnamon, and ginger are just a few of the spices that feature prominently in Grenadian cuisine, earning the island its nickname as the "Spice Isle." These aromatic spices are used to season everything from savory stews and curries to sweet desserts and beverages, adding depth and complexity to traditional Grenadian dishes.

One of the most iconic dishes in Grenadian cuisine is "oil down," a hearty one-pot meal made with salted meat, breadfruit, callaloo (a leafy green vegetable), coconut milk, and a variety of spices. Cooked slowly over an open flame, oil down is a true taste of Grenadian comfort food, beloved by locals and visitors alike for its rich flavors and satisfying texture.

Seafood also plays a prominent role in Grenadian cuisine, thanks to the island's abundant coastal waters and thriving fishing industry. Fresh fish, lobster, shrimp, and crab are commonly enjoyed in

Grenada, prepared in a variety of ways including grilled, fried, steamed, or stewed. One popular seafood dish is "fish broth," a flavorful soup made with fresh fish, vegetables, herbs, and spices, simmered to perfection and served piping hot.

In addition to its savory dishes, Grenada is also famous for its sweet treats and desserts, which showcase the island's tropical fruits and rich culinary heritage. Grenadian desserts often feature ingredients such as coconut, bananas, mangoes, and guavas, combined with spices like nutmeg and cinnamon to create irresistible confections such as coconut drops, banana fritters, and guava cheese.

No discussion of Grenadian cuisine would be complete without mentioning its refreshing beverages, which are as diverse and flavorful as the island's food. Locally brewed beers, such as "Carib" and "Stag," are popular choices among locals and visitors alike, while rum punch and fruit punches made with fresh tropical fruits provide the perfect accompaniment to any meal.

Overall, Grenadian cuisine is a celebration of the island's rich culinary heritage, blending savory spices, fresh seafood, and tropical fruits to create a symphony of flavors that delight the senses and leave a lasting impression. Whether savoring a traditional oil down, indulging in a sweet dessert, or sipping on a refreshing beverage, visitors to Grenada are sure to enjoy a culinary experience that is as vibrant and diverse as the island itself.

Nutmeg and Beyond: The Spice Trade Legacy

The story of nutmeg in Grenada is more than just a tale of spice; it's a narrative of resilience, innovation, and the enduring legacy of the island's spice trade. Nutmeg, a fragrant seed encased in a hard shell, has been prized for centuries for its aromatic flavor and medicinal properties. In the 17th century, Grenada emerged as a major producer of nutmeg, thanks to its fertile soil and ideal climate for spice cultivation.

The cultivation of nutmeg in Grenada began in the late 18th century, when French settlers introduced the crop to the island's fertile soil. The spice flourished in Grenada's tropical climate, and soon became one of the island's most valuable commodities, earning it the nickname "Isle of Spice." Nutmeg quickly became the backbone of Grenada's economy, driving trade and commerce and fueling the island's growth and development.

By the early 19th century, Grenada had become the world's leading producer of nutmeg, supplying over half of the world's supply. The spice trade brought prosperity to the island, attracting immigrants from around the world and transforming Grenada into a vibrant and cosmopolitan hub of commerce and culture.

Nutmeg became synonymous with Grenada, symbolizing the island's identity and heritage.

However, the fortunes of Grenada's nutmeg industry took a dramatic turn in the late 19th century, when a devastating hurricane swept through the island, decimating nutmeg plantations and causing widespread destruction. Despite this setback, Grenadians persevered, rebuilding their nutmeg industry from the ground up and reaffirming their commitment to the spice trade.

In the 20th century, Grenada's nutmeg industry faced new challenges and opportunities, as changes in global trade and agriculture reshaped the dynamics of the spice market. Competition from other nutmeg-producing countries and fluctuations in market demand posed challenges for Grenada's nutmeg farmers, prompting them to innovate and adapt to changing circumstances.

Today, Grenada remains one of the world's leading producers of nutmeg, exporting high-quality spice to markets around the world. The nutmeg industry continues to play a vital role in Grenada's economy, providing livelihoods for thousands of farmers and contributing significantly to the island's GDP.

Beyond nutmeg, Grenada's spice trade legacy extends to other aromatic treasures, including cloves, cinnamon, and ginger, which are also cultivated on the island and prized for their flavor and fragrance. Together, these spices form the cornerstone of Grenada's culinary heritage, infusing its cuisine with a rich tapestry of flavors and aromas that delight the senses and evoke the island's vibrant history and culture.

In summary, Grenada's spice trade legacy is a testament to the island's resilience, ingenuity, and enduring commitment to excellence. From the humble nutmeg seed to the aromatic treasures that grace its shores, Grenada's spice trade heritage continues to shape the island's identity and inspire generations of farmers, artisans, and food lovers around the world.

Exploring Grenada's Beaches: Sun, Sand, and Serenity

Grenada's beaches are among the most beautiful in the Caribbean, with powdery white sand, crystal-clear turquoise waters, and swaying palm trees that beckon travelers to relax and unwind in paradise. From secluded coves to bustling resort areas, Grenada offers a diverse array of beach experiences, each with its own unique charm and allure.

One of the most famous beaches in Grenada is Grand Anse Beach, a two-mile stretch of pristine white sand located just south of the capital city of St. George's. Grand Anse is renowned for its calm, shallow waters and breathtaking views of the surrounding hillsides, making it a popular destination for swimming, sunbathing, and water sports. Visitors to Grand Anse can rent beach chairs and umbrellas, enjoy delicious snacks and drinks from nearby vendors, or simply soak up the sun and watch the world go by. For those seeking a more secluded beach experience, Grenada offers plenty of hidden gems waiting to be discovered. Magazine Beach, located on the southwestern coast of the island, is a tranquil oasis with calm waters and soft sand, perfect for swimming and snorkeling. La Sagesse Beach, nestled along Grenada's southeastern coast, is another hidden treasure, with its lush mangrove forests, gentle waves, and scenic hiking trails that lead to panoramic views of the coastline. Grenada's beaches are not just places to relax and soak up the sun; they also offer a wealth of opportunities for outdoor adventure and exploration. Visitors can try their hand at snorkeling or scuba diving to discover the vibrant coral reefs and marine life that thrive beneath the waves, or embark on a thrilling boat tour to explore the island's hidden coves and offshore islands. Kayaking, paddleboarding, and jet skiing are also popular activities on Grenada's beaches, providing endless opportunities for fun and excitement on the water. In addition to its natural beauty, Grenada's beaches are also steeped in history and culture, with many offering insights into the island's rich heritage and traditions. Levera Beach, located on Grenada's northern coast, is home to a protected nesting site for endangered leatherback turtles, where visitors can witness these majestic creatures laying their eggs under the cover of night. Bathway Beach, on the northeastern tip of the island, is known for its natural rock formations and tranquil swimming lagoon, as well as its proximity to the historic Belmont Estate, a former sugar plantation turned cultural heritage site. Whether seeking relaxation, adventure, or cultural enrichment, Grenada's beaches offer something for everyone, inviting visitors to experience the sun, sand, and serenity of this idyllic Caribbean destination. From its world-famous stretches of sand to its hidden coves and pristine bays, Grenada's beaches are a true treasure trove waiting to be explored and enjoyed by all who visit.

Underwater Wonders: Diving and Snorkeling Hotspots

Beneath the surface of Grenada's turquoise waters lies a hidden world of wonders, waiting to be discovered by adventurous divers and snorkelers. With its vibrant coral reefs, colorful marine life, and fascinating underwater landscapes, Grenada offers some of the best diving and snorkeling experiences in the Caribbean.

One of the most popular diving destinations in Grenada is the Molinere Underwater Sculpture Park, located just off the coast of St. George's. Created by British sculptor Jason deCaires Taylor, the park is home to a stunning collection of submerged sculptures that serve as artificial reefs, providing habitat for a diverse array of marine life. Divers can explore the sculptures up close, marveling at their intricate details and the unique ecosystems they support.

Another must-visit diving site in Grenada is the Bianca C, also known as the "Titanic of the Caribbean." This massive wreck, which lies in shallow waters off the coast of St. George's, is one of the largest and most accessible shipwrecks in the Caribbean, attracting divers from around the world. The wreck is home to a rich variety of marine life, including colorful corals, tropical fish, and even the occasional reef shark.

For snorkelers, Grenada offers countless opportunities to explore its vibrant coral reefs and underwater landscapes. One popular snorkeling spot is Flamingo Bay, located on the southwestern coast of the island. Here, snorkelers can swim among colorful coral gardens, spotting tropical fish, sea turtles, and other marine creatures as they explore the shallow waters of the bay.

Another fantastic snorkeling destination in Grenada is the Underwater Sculpture Park, where snorkelers can swim above the submerged sculptures and observe them from the surface. This unique experience offers a glimpse into the world of underwater art and provides a fascinating opportunity to witness the interaction between art and nature.

Grenada's underwater wonders are not limited to its coastlines; the island also boasts several offshore reefs and dive sites that are accessible by boat. The Grenada Marine Park, located off the southern coast of the island, is home to a network of protected reefs and dive sites that offer some of the best diving in the Caribbean. Here, divers can explore coral-encrusted walls, swim-throughs, and underwater pinnacles teeming with life.

Whether diving among shipwrecks, exploring underwater sculptures, or snorkeling over coral reefs, Grenada offers an unparalleled opportunity to experience the beauty and diversity of the underwater world. With its clear waters, abundant marine life, and variety of dive sites, Grenada is truly a diver's paradise, beckoning adventurers to dive in and discover the wonders that lie beneath the surface.

Waterfalls and Hiking Trails: Discovering Grenada's Interior

Grenada's interior is a lush and verdant paradise, filled with hidden waterfalls, cascading rivers, and verdant hiking trails waiting to be explored. Nestled amid the island's rugged mountains and dense rainforests, these natural wonders offer a glimpse into Grenada's wild and untamed beauty, providing a welcome escape from the hustle and bustle of modern life.

One of the most iconic waterfalls in Grenada is Annandale Falls, located just a short drive from the capital city of St. George's. This picturesque waterfall cascades down a series of rocky cliffs into a crystal-clear pool below, surrounded by lush tropical vegetation and towering bamboo trees. Visitors can swim in the refreshing waters of the pool, take in the stunning views from the observation deck, or simply relax and enjoy the tranquil atmosphere of this natural oasis.

Another must-visit waterfall in Grenada is Concord Falls, located in the island's interior near the village of Concord. This series of three waterfalls, known as Concord Upper, Concord Middle, and Concord Lower, are nestled amid the lush rainforest of Grenada's interior, accessible via a scenic hike through the forest. Each waterfall offers its own unique beauty and charm, with refreshing pools and cascading streams that invite visitors to take a refreshing dip and immerse themselves in nature. For those seeking a more adventurous hiking experience, Grenada offers a network of scenic trails that wind through its mountains, valleys, and forests. One popular hiking destination is Grand Etang National Park, located in the heart of the island. Here, visitors can explore a variety of hiking trails that lead to stunning viewpoints, hidden waterfalls, and serene crater lakes, providing a glimpse into Grenada's rich natural heritage.

Another fantastic hiking destination in Grenada is Mt. Qua Qua, a challenging yet rewarding trail that leads to the summit of one of the island's highest peaks. Along the way, hikers will encounter breathtaking vistas, lush rainforest vegetation, and a variety of wildlife, including colorful birds and playful monkeys. At the summit, hikers are rewarded with panoramic views of Grenada's coastline and interior, making it the perfect spot to pause and take in the beauty of the island.

In addition to its waterfalls and hiking trails, Grenada's interior is also home to a variety of cultural and historical attractions, including ancient Amerindian petroglyphs, traditional cocoa plantations, and quaint mountain villages. Exploring Grenada's interior is a journey of discovery, offering travelers the chance to connect with nature, immerse themselves in local culture, and create memories that will last a lifetime.

Grenada's National Parks: Preserving Natural Treasures

Grenada's national parks are the guardians of the island's natural treasures, preserving its rich biodiversity and protecting its pristine landscapes for future generations to enjoy. These protected areas encompass a variety of ecosystems, from lush rainforests and rugged mountains to pristine coastline and vibrant coral reefs, offering visitors the chance to explore and appreciate Grenada's stunning natural beauty up close.

One of the most iconic national parks in Grenada is Grand Etang National Park, located in the island's interior. This sprawling park encompasses over 3,800 acres of tropical rainforest, volcanic crater lakes, and scenic hiking trails, making it a haven for nature lovers and outdoor enthusiasts. Within the park, visitors can explore a network of trails that wind through dense forest, past cascading waterfalls, and up to panoramic viewpoints that offer breathtaking vistas of the surrounding landscape. Another notable national park in Grenada is Levera National Park, located on the island's northern coast. This coastal park protects a diverse range of habitats, including mangrove forests, salt marshes, and sandy beaches, as well as nesting sites for endangered leatherback turtles. Visitors to Levera National Park can explore its scenic trails, enjoy birdwatching and wildlife spotting opportunities, or simply relax on its pristine beaches and take in the serene beauty of the coastline. Grenada is also home to several marine protected areas, which safeguard its valuable coral reefs and marine ecosystems from overfishing, pollution, and other threats. The Moliniere-Beausejour Marine Protected Area, located off the coast of St. George's, is one such area, offering snorkelers and divers the chance to explore its vibrant coral reefs and underwater sculptures while helping to conserve and protect these fragile habitats. In addition to its natural beauty, Grenada's national parks are also important centers of research and education, providing valuable opportunities for scientists, students, and conservationists to study and learn about the island's unique ecosystems. Many national parks in Grenada offer interpretive programs, guided tours, and educational exhibits that help visitors better understand the importance of conservation and the role they can play in protecting Grenada's natural heritage.

Overall, Grenada's national parks are a testament to the island's commitment to conservation and sustainable development, ensuring that its natural treasures remain intact for future generations to enjoy. Whether hiking through dense rainforest, snorkeling on vibrant coral reefs, or simply soaking up the serenity of a secluded beach, visitors to Grenada's national parks are sure to be captivated by the beauty and diversity of this idyllic Caribbean destination.

Carriacou: A Gem within a Gem

Carriacou, often referred to as the "Isle of Reefs," is a hidden gem nestled within the heart of the Grenadines, just a short ferry ride from mainland Grenada. Despite its small size, measuring only 13 square miles, Carriacou boasts a rich cultural heritage, stunning natural beauty, and laid-back atmosphere that beckons travelers to explore its shores and immerse themselves in its charm.

The history of Carriacou is as diverse and colorful as the island itself, shaped by centuries of indigenous settlement, European colonization, and African influences. The island was originally inhabited by the Kalinago people, who called it "Kayryouacou," meaning "land of reefs." In the 18th century, Carriacou became a strategic outpost for the British Empire, serving as a center for trade and commerce in the Caribbean. Today, Carriacou is home to a vibrant community of around 8,000 residents, who are known for their warmth, hospitality, and strong sense of community. The island's main town, Hillsborough, is a bustling hub of activity, with colorful shops, bustling markets, and lively waterfront bars where locals and visitors alike gather to socialize and unwind. Despite its small size, Carriacou offers a wealth of attractions and activities for visitors to enjoy. One of the island's main draws is its stunning beaches, which boast powdery white sand, clear turquoise waters, and pristine coral reefs teeming with marine life.

Paradise Beach, located on the northern coast of the island, is a favorite among visitors, offering excellent snorkeling and swimming opportunities in a tranquil and secluded setting. In addition to its beaches, Carriacou is also known for its vibrant cultural scene, with a rich tradition of music, dance, and storytelling that reflects the island's African, European, and indigenous roots. The annual Carriacou Maroon and String Band Music Festival, held every April, is a highlight of the island's cultural calendar, featuring live performances by local musicians, traditional dance troupes, and colorful parades that celebrate Carriacou's unique heritage. For those interested in history and heritage, Carriacou offers several fascinating attractions to explore, including the Carriacou Museum, which showcases the island's history, culture, and natural heritage through a collection of artifacts, photographs, and exhibits. Visitors can also explore historic sites such as the Gun Point Battery, a 19th-century British military fortification that offers panoramic views of the surrounding coastline.

In summary, Carriacou is a true gem within the gem of Grenada, offering visitors a glimpse into the authentic Caribbean experience with its stunning beaches, vibrant culture, and rich history. Whether snorkeling on its coral reefs, dancing to the rhythm of its music, or exploring its historic sites, visitors to Carriacou are sure to be captivated by the island's beauty and charm.

Petite Martinique: The Quintessential Caribbean Escape

Nestled among the turquoise waters of the Grenadines lies Petite Martinique, a tiny island paradise that embodies the essence of the Caribbean escape. Measuring just over a mile in length, Petite Martinique is the smallest of the three inhabited islands in the nation of Grenada, yet it packs a big punch when it comes to natural beauty, laid-back charm, and authentic island living.

Despite its small size, Petite Martinique boasts a rich history and cultural heritage that is deeply intertwined with the sea. For centuries, the island has been a center for boat-building and seafaring, with its residents renowned for their skills in crafting traditional wooden boats known as "sloops." Today, the art of boat-building remains an integral part of life on Petite Martinique, with local craftsmen continuing to produce these iconic vessels using traditional methods passed down through generations.

Petite Martinique's rugged coastline is dotted with secluded coves, hidden beaches, and pristine coral reefs, making it a haven for snorkelers, divers, and beach lovers alike. The island's main beach, aptly named "Palm Beach," is a tranquil stretch of golden sand fringed by swaying palm trees and crystal-clear waters, offering the perfect spot to relax and soak up the sun in peace and solitude.

In addition to its natural beauty, Petite Martinique is also known for its vibrant community spirit and warm hospitality. The island's small population of around 900 residents is known for its strong sense of community, with neighbors looking out for one another and visitors always receiving a warm welcome. The island's main settlement, known simply as "The Village," is a charming cluster of colorful houses, local shops, and friendly faces, where visitors can immerse themselves in the laid-back rhythm of island life.

Despite its remote location, Petite Martinique offers a surprising array of amenities and activities for visitors to enjoy. The island is home to several guesthouses and small hotels, as well as restaurants serving up delicious local cuisine and fresh seafood caught daily by local fishermen. Visitors can also explore the island's rugged interior on foot, hiking along scenic trails that offer panoramic views of the surrounding sea and neighboring islands.

For those seeking adventure, Petite Martinique offers plenty of opportunities to get out on the water and explore its pristine marine environment. Visitors can charter a boat to explore nearby uninhabited islands and secluded beaches, or try their hand at fishing for marlin, tuna, and other game fish that abound in the waters surrounding the island.

In summary, Petite Martinique is the quintessential Caribbean escape, offering visitors the chance to experience the beauty, tranquility, and authentic island culture of the Grenadines in its purest form. Whether relaxing on its secluded beaches, exploring its rugged coastline, or immersing oneself in its vibrant community life, a visit to Petite Martinique is sure to leave a lasting impression and create memories that will be cherished for a lifetime.

St. George's: A Historic and Picturesque Capital

St. George's, the capital of Grenada, is a city steeped in history and brimming with charm. Nestled on the southwestern coast of the island, St. George's is renowned for its colorful colonial architecture, picturesque harbor, and vibrant cultural scene, making it a must-visit destination for travelers exploring the Caribbean.

The city's history dates back to the 17th century when it was founded by the French as Fort Royal. Over the centuries, St. George's has changed hands multiple times, passing from French to British control before finally gaining independence as part of the nation of Grenada in 1974. Today, traces of the city's colonial past can still be seen in its historic buildings, cobblestone streets, and quaint alleyways, which evoke a sense of old-world charm and nostalgia.

One of the most iconic landmarks in St. George's is Fort George, a historic military fortress perched on a hill overlooking the city and its picturesque harbor. Built by the French in the early 18th century and later expanded by the British, Fort George offers panoramic views of St. George's and the surrounding coastline, making it a popular spot for visitors to take in the beauty of the city and its surroundings. In addition to its historic architecture, St. George's is also known for its vibrant marketplaces, where locals and visitors alike gather to buy and sell fresh produce, spices, crafts, and souvenirs. The Market Square, located in the heart of the city, is a bustling hub of activity, with vendors hawking their wares amid the colorful stalls and lively atmosphere.

St. George's is also home to a rich cultural scene, with numerous art galleries, museums, and theaters showcasing the island's vibrant arts and music scene. The Grenada National Museum, located in a historic building near the harbor, offers visitors a glimpse into the island's history and culture through its collection of artifacts, photographs, and exhibits.

One of the highlights of St. George's is its picturesque waterfront, where colorful buildings line the harbor and fishing boats bob gently in the breeze. The Carenage, a horseshoe-shaped harbor that forms the centerpiece of the city, is a popular spot for strolling, dining, and enjoying the sunset over the Caribbean Sea.

Despite its small size, St. George's offers plenty of amenities and attractions for visitors to enjoy, including boutique hotels, cozy guesthouses, and a variety of restaurants serving up delicious local cuisine and international fare. Whether exploring its historic streets, soaking up the sun on its beautiful beaches, or simply taking in the sights and sounds of the city, a visit to St. George's is sure to be an unforgettable experience.

History Comes Alive: Forts and Museums of Grenada

Exploring the forts and museums of Grenada is like stepping back in time to experience the island's rich and diverse history firsthand. From ancient Amerindian settlements to colonial-era fortifications and cultural heritage sites, Grenada's historical landmarks offer a fascinating glimpse into the island's past and its enduring legacy.

One of the most iconic historical sites in Grenada is Fort George, perched atop a hill overlooking the capital city of St. George's and its picturesque harbor. Built by the French in the early 18th century and later expanded by the British, Fort George played a crucial role in the island's defense during periods of colonial rule. Today, visitors to Fort George can explore its well-preserved ramparts, cannons, and barracks, and enjoy panoramic views of St. George's and the surrounding coastline. Another must-visit historical landmark in Grenada is Fort Frederick, located on Richmond Hill overlooking the capital. Built by the French in the late 18th century and later occupied by the British, Fort Frederick offers commanding views of St. George's and its harbor, as well as the surrounding countryside. The fort is named after Frederick, Duke of York, the second son of King George III, who served as Commander-in-Chief of the British Army during the Napoleonic Wars. In addition to its forts,

Grenada is also home to several museums that offer insights into the island's history, culture, and natural heritage. The Grenada National Museum, located in the capital city of St. George's, houses a diverse collection of artifacts, photographs, and exhibits that tell the story of Grenada's past, from its Amerindian inhabitants to its colonial history and struggle for independence. Highlights of the museum's collection include artifacts from the island's indigenous peoples, colonial-era relics, and exhibits on Grenada's rich cultural traditions, including music, dance, and cuisine. Another museum worth visiting in Grenada is the Belmont Estate Heritage Museum, located in the parish of St. Patrick's. This historic plantation estate offers visitors the chance to learn about Grenada's agricultural heritage, including the cultivation of cocoa, nutmeg, and other spices that have shaped the island's economy and culture for centuries. The museum features exhibits on the history of the estate, as well as demonstrations of traditional farming methods and processing techniques.

In addition to these historical landmarks, Grenada is also home to numerous other sites of historical significance, including ancient Amerindian petroglyphs, colonial-era churches, and plantation estates. Whether exploring the ramparts of a centuries-old fort, delving into the island's colonial past at a museum, or discovering the secrets of Grenada's agricultural heritage at a historic estate, visitors to Grenada are sure to be captivated by the island's rich history and cultural heritage.

Grenadian Festivals: Celebrating Culture and Tradition

Grenadian festivals are vibrant celebrations of culture, tradition, and community spirit that showcase the island's rich heritage and diversity. From colorful parades and lively music to delicious food and traditional dances, these festivals offer visitors a unique opportunity to immerse themselves in the sights, sounds, and flavors of Grenada's vibrant cultural scene.

One of the most famous festivals in Grenada is the annual Spice Mas, held every August to celebrate the island's abundant spice crops and vibrant cultural heritage. The festival kicks off with a spectacular opening parade, featuring elaborate costumes, colorful floats, and pulsating rhythms that fill the streets of St. George's with energy and excitement. Throughout the week-long celebration, visitors can enjoy a variety of events and activities, including calypso competitions, steel pan performances, and traditional masquerade dances known as "Jab Jab."

Another highlight of the Grenadian festival calendar is the Carriacou Maroon and String Band Music Festival, held every April on the sister island of Carriacou. This unique festival celebrates the island's African heritage and musical traditions, with live performances by local string bands, drummers, and dancers who entertain crowds with

45

their infectious rhythms and spirited performances. The festival also features cultural workshops, craft displays, and traditional games, providing visitors with a glimpse into the island's rich cultural heritage.

In addition to these larger festivals, Grenada is also home to a variety of smaller, community-based celebrations that highlight the island's diverse cultural influences. The Fisherman's Birthday, held annually in the fishing village of Gouyave, is a lively street party that honors the island's fishermen with music, dancing, and plenty of fresh seafood. The La Baye Folk Festival, held in the rural parish of St. John's, celebrates Grenada's African and French heritage with traditional music, dance, and storytelling.

Grenadian festivals are not just about entertainment; they also play an important role in preserving and promoting the island's cultural traditions and heritage. Many festivals feature traditional crafts, culinary demonstrations, and cultural exhibits that educate visitors about Grenada's history, customs, and way of life. Whether sampling local delicacies at a food fair, learning traditional dance moves at a cultural workshop, or joining in the festivities at a street party, visitors to Grenada's festivals are sure to be captivated by the island's rich cultural tapestry and warm hospitality.

Music and Dance: Vibrant Rhythms of the Spice Isle

Music and dance are integral parts of Grenada's cultural identity, infusing the island with vibrant rhythms and infectious energy that reflect its diverse heritage and traditions. From traditional drumming and folk dances to modern genres like soca and reggae, Grenada's music scene is as diverse as it is dynamic, offering something for everyone to enjoy.

One of the most iconic musical traditions in Grenada is calypso, a genre that originated in the Caribbean and is characterized by its witty lyrics, catchy melodies, and infectious rhythms. Calypso music has deep roots in Grenada's history, dating back to the days of slavery when enslaved Africans used music as a form of expression and resistance. Today, calypso remains a popular genre in Grenada, with local artists known as "calypsonians" performing at festivals, competitions, and other cultural events throughout the year.

Another popular musical tradition in Grenada is steel pan, a percussive art form that originated in Trinidad and Tobago and has since spread throughout the Caribbean. Steel pan music is characterized by its melodic tones and intricate rhythms, which are produced by striking metal

47

drums of various sizes with mallets or sticks. In Grenada, steel pan bands can be found performing at festivals, street parties, and other cultural events, delighting audiences with their skillful performances and infectious grooves.

Soca music is another genre that holds a special place in Grenada's musical landscape, particularly during the annual Spice Mas festival. Originating in Trinidad and Tobago, soca is a lively and energetic genre that blends elements of calypso, African rhythms, and Western pop music. During Spice Mas, soca music fills the streets of St. George's, as revelers dance in colorful costumes and celebrate the island's vibrant culture and heritage.

In addition to these traditional genres, Grenada is also home to a thriving reggae music scene, with local artists putting their own spin on this iconic genre made famous by Jamaican legends like Bob Marley and Peter Tosh. Reggae music can be heard at bars, clubs, and live music venues throughout the island, with local bands and musicians performing both classic hits and original compositions that reflect Grenada's unique cultural identity.

Dance is also an integral part of Grenada's cultural heritage, with traditional folk dances like the Bele and the Quadrille preserving the island's African, French, and British influences. These dances are often performed at weddings, festivals, and other special occasions, with dancers clad in colorful costumes and accompanied by live drumming and music.

Overall, music and dance are central to Grenada's cultural identity, serving as a source of pride, joy, and expression for its people. Whether celebrating at a festival, dancing to the beat of a steel pan band, or simply enjoying the sounds of reggae drifting through the air, visitors to Grenada are sure to be captivated by the island's vibrant rhythms and infectious energy.

The Artistic Heritage of Grenada: Craftsmanship and Creativity

The artistic heritage of Grenada is a rich tapestry woven with craftsmanship, creativity, and cultural expression. From intricate woodcarvings and vibrant paintings to exquisite pottery and handmade textiles, Grenadian artisans showcase their talents and traditions through a diverse range of artistic mediums.

One of the most celebrated forms of artistic expression in Grenada is woodcarving, a craft that has been practiced on the island for centuries. Grenadian woodcarvers are renowned for their skillful craftsmanship and attention to detail, creating intricate sculptures, masks, and furniture that reflect the island's natural beauty and cultural heritage. Many woodcarvers draw inspiration from Grenada's lush rainforests and diverse wildlife, incorporating motifs such as tropical flowers, birds, and sea creatures into their designs.

In addition to woodcarving, Grenada is also known for its vibrant painting tradition, with local artists capturing the island's stunning landscapes, colorful street scenes, and vibrant culture on canvas. The island's art galleries showcase a diverse range of styles and techniques, from realistic landscapes and portraits to abstract and contemporary works that push the boundaries of artistic expression. Many Grenadian artists draw inspiration from the island's natural beauty, vibrant colors, and rich cultural heritage, creating artworks that resonate with both locals and visitors alike.

Pottery is another traditional craft that thrives in Grenada, with local potters creating beautiful and functional pieces using techniques that have been passed down through generations. Grenadian pottery is characterized by its earthy tones, organic shapes, and unique decorative motifs, reflecting the island's connection to the land and its rich cultural heritage. Visitors to Grenada can explore pottery studios and workshops, where they can watch skilled artisans at work and purchase one-of-a-kind pieces to take home as souvenirs.

Textile arts also play an important role in Grenada's artistic heritage, with local weavers and seamstresses creating beautiful fabrics and garments using traditional techniques such as batik and weaving. Grenadian textiles are known for their bold colors, intricate patterns, and high-quality craftsmanship, with many artisans drawing inspiration from the island's natural landscapes, flora, and fauna. Visitors to Grenada can explore local markets and boutiques, where they can purchase handmade clothing, accessories, and home decor items that showcase the island's rich textile traditions.

Overall, the artistic heritage of Grenada is a testament to the island's creativity, craftsmanship, and cultural diversity. Whether exploring a woodcarver's workshop, admiring a local artist's painting, or browsing through a pottery studio, visitors to Grenada are sure to be inspired by the island's vibrant artistic scene and the talent and passion of its artisans.

Religion and Spirituality: Diverse Beliefs in Harmony

Religion and spirituality in Grenada reflect the island's rich cultural tapestry and diverse population, with a harmonious blend of beliefs and practices that coexist peacefully. The predominant religion in Grenada is Christianity, with the majority of the population identifying as Catholic, Anglican, or Protestant. These Christian denominations have deep historical roots in Grenada, dating back to the colonial era when European settlers introduced Christianity to the island.

Catholicism is the largest Christian denomination in Grenada, with a significant number of Grenadians identifying as Catholics and attending mass at the island's numerous Catholic churches. The Catholic Church has played an important role in Grenadian society, providing spiritual guidance, education, and social services to its members and the wider community.

In addition to Catholicism, Anglicanism is also a prominent Christian denomination in Grenada, with Anglican churches scattered throughout the island. The Anglican Church has a long history in Grenada, dating back to the 18th century when the British established Anglican missions on the island. Today, Anglican churches in Grenada continue to serve as centers of worship and community life, hosting regular services, religious ceremonies, and social events.

Protestantism is another major branch of Christianity in Grenada, with a diverse array of Protestant denominations represented on the island, including Methodist, Baptist, Pentecostal, and Seventh-day Adventist churches. These Protestant churches attract large congregations of worshippers who come together to pray, sing hymns, and participate in religious activities that strengthen their faith and sense of community.

In addition to Christianity, Grenada is also home to small but vibrant communities of Hindus, Muslims, and followers of other religious traditions. Hinduism, brought to Grenada by indentured laborers from India in the 19th century, is practiced by a small but devout community who celebrate festivals such as Diwali and Holi with colorful rituals and ceremonies.

Islam is also practiced by a small but growing community of Muslims in Grenada, who gather for prayer, study, and religious observance at mosques located throughout the island. The Muslim community in Grenada is known for its hospitality and inclusivity, welcoming visitors of all backgrounds to learn about Islam and participate in community events.

Overall, religion and spirituality in Grenada are characterized by a spirit of tolerance, acceptance, and mutual respect, with people of different faiths living and worshiping together in harmony. The diverse array of religious beliefs and practices in Grenada enriches the island's cultural landscape and contributes to its sense of identity and unity as a nation.

Language and Linguistic Heritage: The Melody of Creole

Language and linguistic heritage in Grenada are as diverse and colorful as the island itself, with a rich tapestry of languages and dialects reflecting its history, culture, and multicultural heritage. While English is the official language of Grenada and widely spoken and understood throughout the island, it is the local Grenadian Creole that truly embodies the unique linguistic identity of the nation.

Grenadian Creole, also known as Grenadian Patois or simply "Patois," is a creole language that evolved from a combination of West African languages, French, English, and indigenous Caribbean languages spoken by enslaved Africans and their descendants during the colonial era. Over time, Grenadian Creole developed its own distinct vocabulary, grammar, and pronunciation, influenced by the linguistic traditions of the various cultural groups that inhabited the island.

Grenadian Creole is characterized by its melodic cadence, expressive intonation, and colorful vocabulary, which draws from a diverse range of linguistic influences. While English serves as the primary language of formal communication and education in Grenada, Grenadian Creole is the language of everyday conversation, informal interaction, and cultural expression among the local population.

One of the defining features of Grenadian Creole is its use of "code-switching," wherein speakers seamlessly alternate between English and Creole depending on the social context, audience, and communicative purpose. This fluidity between languages reflects the dynamic and adaptive nature of Grenadian Creole, which continues to evolve and thrive as a living language spoken by Grenadians of all ages and backgrounds.

In addition to Grenadian Creole, Grenada is also home to small communities of speakers of other languages, including French and Spanish, which reflect the island's colonial history and multicultural heritage. While these languages are not as widely spoken as English and Creole, they contribute to the linguistic diversity of Grenada and enrich the island's cultural landscape.

Overall, language and linguistic heritage in Grenada are integral components of the island's identity and sense of belonging, with Grenadian Creole serving as a powerful symbol of cultural resilience, solidarity, and pride. Whether engaging in lively conversation with locals, enjoying the rhythmic cadences of Creole music, or savoring the flavors of Creole cuisine, visitors to Grenada are sure to be captivated by the melodic charm and linguistic richness of the Spice Isle.

Education in Grenada: Nurturing Minds for the Future

Education in Grenada plays a vital role in shaping the future of the nation by nurturing young minds, fostering critical thinking, and empowering individuals to achieve their full potential. The education system in Grenada follows a model based on the British system, with primary, secondary, and tertiary levels of education.

At the primary level, children in Grenada typically start school at around the age of five and attend primary school for six years. Primary education is free and compulsory for all children, and schools follow a standardized curriculum that covers core subjects such as English, mathematics, science, social studies, and physical education. In addition to academic subjects, primary schools in Grenada also emphasize character development, creativity, and social skills, preparing students for success in secondary education and beyond.

Secondary education in Grenada consists of two levels: lower secondary (grades 7-9) and upper secondary (grades 10-11 or 12). Students are assessed through the Caribbean Secondary Education Certificate (CSEC) examinations at the end of grade 11, which determine their eligibility for further education or entry into the workforce. The curriculum at the secondary level is more specialized, with students having the opportunity to choose elective subjects based on their interests and career goals.

In addition to traditional academic subjects, secondary schools in Grenada also offer technical and vocational education programs that provide students with practical skills and training in areas such as agriculture, hospitality, and trades. These programs are designed to prepare students for careers in industries that are vital to Grenada's economy and contribute to the island's sustainable development.

At the tertiary level, Grenada is home to several institutions of higher education, including the T.A. Marryshow Community College (TAMCC) and the St. George's University (SGU). TAMCC offers a range of associate degree and certificate programs in fields such as business, engineering, health sciences, and liberal arts, providing students with opportunities for further education and career advancement.

St. George's University is a private international university that offers undergraduate and graduate programs in medicine, veterinary medicine, public health, and other health sciences. With its state-of-the-art facilities, renowned faculty, and diverse student body, SGU attracts students from across the globe who come to Grenada to pursue their dreams of becoming healthcare professionals and making a positive impact on the world.

Overall, education in Grenada is focused on providing students with a well-rounded education that prepares them for success in an increasingly globalized and competitive world. By investing in the future of its young people, Grenada is laying the foundation for a prosperous and sustainable future for generations to come.

Economy and Industry: Beyond the Nutmeg Trade

Grenada's economy and industry have evolved significantly over the years, moving beyond its traditional reliance on the nutmeg trade to embrace new sectors and opportunities for growth. While nutmeg and other spices remain important exports for Grenada, the island's economy has diversified to include tourism, agriculture, manufacturing, and services.

The nutmeg trade has long been the backbone of Grenada's economy, earning the island its nickname as the "Spice Isle." Grenada is one of the world's largest producers of nutmeg and mace, with the spice industry contributing significantly to the island's GDP and providing employment opportunities for thousands of Grenadians. Nutmeg and other spices are grown primarily in the mountainous interior of the island, where the fertile soil and tropical climate provide ideal conditions for cultivation.

In recent years, however, Grenada has recognized the need to diversify its economy and reduce its dependence on the nutmeg trade. Tourism has emerged as a key driver of economic growth, with the island's stunning beaches, lush rainforests, and vibrant cultural heritage attracting visitors from around the world. The tourism industry in Grenada encompasses a wide range of activities, including eco-tourism, adventure tourism, and luxury tourism, catering to diverse interests and preferences.

Agriculture remains an important sector of Grenada's economy, with farmers cultivating a variety of crops, including bananas, cocoa, citrus fruits, and vegetables, for both domestic consumption and export. Grenada is also known for its thriving fishing industry, with fishermen harvesting a variety of seafood, including lobster, tuna, and shrimp, for local markets and export to other countries in the Caribbean and beyond.

Manufacturing is another growing sector of Grenada's economy, with companies producing a variety of goods, including food and beverages, textiles, and pharmaceuticals, for domestic consumption and export. The government of Grenada has implemented policies to promote investment and create a business-friendly environment to attract foreign investment and stimulate economic growth in the manufacturing sector.

Services such as banking, finance, and information technology are also playing an increasingly important role in Grenada's economy, with the island emerging as a regional hub for financial services and technology innovation. The government has implemented initiatives to promote entrepreneurship, innovation, and digital literacy to support the growth of the services sector and create new opportunities for Grenadians.

Overall, Grenada's economy and industry are dynamic and diverse, with the island embracing new opportunities for growth and development while preserving its rich cultural heritage and natural resources. By leveraging its strengths and embracing innovation, Grenada is positioning itself for a prosperous and sustainable future in the global economy.

Government and Politics: Democratic Principles in Action

Grenada's government and politics are grounded in democratic principles, with a system of governance that promotes accountability, transparency, and the rule of law. The country operates under a parliamentary democracy, with a constitutional monarchy and a Westminster-style parliamentary system of government. The head of state is the monarch of the United Kingdom, represented in Grenada by a Governor-General who serves as the ceremonial representative of the Crown.

The real executive power in Grenada lies with the Prime Minister, who is the head of government and leads the Cabinet, responsible for making policy decisions and implementing government programs. The Prime Minister is typically the leader of the political party that commands the majority of seats in the House of Representatives, the lower house of Parliament. Members of Parliament are elected by the people of Grenada through a system of universal suffrage, with elections held every five years.

The Parliament of Grenada is bicameral, consisting of two chambers: the House of Representatives and the Senate. The House of Representatives is made up of elected members who represent constituencies across the country, while the Senate is composed of members appointed by the Governor-General on the advice of the Prime Minister and the Leader of the Opposition. The Parliament is responsible for making laws, debating national issues, and scrutinizing the actions of the government.

Grenada's legal system is based on English common law, with a strong emphasis on the protection of individual rights and freedoms. The judiciary is independent and impartial, ensuring that the rule of law is upheld and that justice is administered fairly and transparently. The highest court in Grenada is the Eastern Caribbean Supreme Court, which consists of the Court of Appeal and the High Court. Appeals from the Eastern Caribbean Supreme Court can be further heard by the Judicial Committee of the Privy Council in London, the final court of appeal for Grenada.

In addition to its domestic affairs, Grenada is also an active member of the international community, participating in regional and international organizations such as the Caribbean Community (CARICOM), the Organization of Eastern Caribbean States (OECS), and the United Nations (UN). Grenada's foreign policy is guided by principles of sovereignty, non-interference, and cooperation, with a focus on promoting peace, security, and sustainable development in the region and beyond.

Overall, Grenada's government and politics reflect a commitment to democratic values and principles, with institutions and processes in place to ensure the participation of citizens in decision-making, the protection of their rights and freedoms, and the promotion of good governance and accountability. By upholding these democratic principles, Grenada continues to strengthen its political stability and foster a climate of trust, confidence, and progress for its people and its future.

Healthcare and Wellness: Holistic Approaches to Well-being

Healthcare and wellness in Grenada are approached with a focus on holistic well-being, incorporating both traditional and modern practices to promote physical, mental, and spiritual health. The healthcare system in Grenada is based on a combination of public and private healthcare facilities, providing accessible and affordable medical services to the population.

The Ministry of Health oversees the healthcare system in Grenada, responsible for developing health policies, regulating healthcare providers, and delivering essential health services to the public. The government operates a network of public health facilities, including hospitals, clinics, and health centers, that provide a wide range of services, from primary care and preventive medicine to specialized treatment and emergency care.

Grenada's public healthcare system is supplemented by a growing private healthcare sector, which offers additional options for patients seeking medical care. Private hospitals, clinics, and specialist practices provide a range of services, including elective surgery, diagnostic imaging, and specialized medical treatment, catering to both local residents and medical tourists from abroad.

In addition to conventional medical care, Grenada also embraces traditional and alternative healing practices that are rooted in the island's cultural heritage and natural resources. Herbal medicine, for example, is widely used in Grenada for treating common ailments and promoting overall wellness. Local herbs and plants such as lemongrass, soursop, and moringa are valued for their medicinal properties and are incorporated into teas, tinctures, and topical remedies.

Grenada's natural environment also provides opportunities for outdoor recreation and activities that promote physical fitness and mental well-being. The island's lush rainforests, pristine beaches, and crystal-clear waters offer opportunities for hiking, swimming, snorkeling, and other outdoor pursuits that promote physical activity and stress relief.

Mental health and wellness are also prioritized in Grenada, with efforts to raise awareness, reduce stigma, and improve access to mental health services. The government, in collaboration with local organizations and international partners, has implemented initiatives to provide counseling, support services, and treatment for mental health conditions, recognizing the importance of emotional and psychological well-being in overall health.

Overall, healthcare and wellness in Grenada are approached with a holistic perspective, recognizing the interconnectedness of mind, body, and spirit. By embracing a combination of traditional and modern practices, Grenada seeks to empower individuals to take control of their health and well-being and lead fulfilling and balanced lives.

Transportation in Grenada: Navigating the Island's Terrain

Transportation in Grenada presents a unique set of challenges and opportunities due to the island's varied terrain, lush landscapes, and coastal geography. While Grenada is relatively small in size, spanning just 133 square miles, its mountainous terrain and winding roads can make travel within the island both scenic and challenging.

One of the primary modes of transportation in Grenada is the road network, which consists of a network of paved roads that connect the island's towns, villages, and tourist attractions. The main highway, known as the Maurice Bishop Highway, runs along the western coast of the island, providing access to the capital city of St. George's and other major towns. While the main roads are generally well-maintained, some secondary roads and rural routes may be narrow and winding, requiring careful navigation, especially for drivers unfamiliar with the terrain.

Driving is the most common way to get around Grenada, with many visitors opting to rent cars or scooters to explore the island at their own pace. Rental agencies are available in major towns and at the airport, offering a range of vehicles to suit different preferences and budgets. It's important to note that driving is done on the left side of the road in Grenada, following British road rules, and seat belts are required by law.

Public transportation options in Grenada include buses, taxis, and minivans, which provide affordable and convenient transportation for locals and visitors alike. Buses operate on set routes throughout the island, with designated stops and fixed fares, making them a popular choice for commuters and travelers looking to explore Grenada on a budget. Taxis are also readily available and can be hailed on the street or booked in advance for longer journeys or tours.

For travelers looking to explore Grenada's coastal areas and neighboring islands, ferry services are available to connect the main island with Carriacou and Petite Martinique. The Osprey Lines ferry operates regular services between Grenada and Carriacou, with crossings taking approximately two hours. Ferries provide an affordable and scenic way to travel between the islands, offering stunning views of the Caribbean Sea and the Grenadine archipelago.

In addition to land and sea transportation, Grenada also has a small international airport, the Maurice Bishop International Airport

(MBIA), located just outside of St. George's. The airport serves as the main gateway to the island, with regular flights to and from destinations in the Caribbean, North America, Europe, and beyond. Domestic flights are also available between Grenada and Carriacou, providing convenient air travel options for inter-island connections.

Overall, transportation in Grenada offers a variety of options for getting around the island, whether by road, sea, or air. With its diverse landscapes, scenic routes, and friendly locals, navigating Grenada's terrain is an adventure in itself, offering travelers an unforgettable experience of the Spice Isle.

Hospitality and Accommodation: Where to Stay and What to Expect

Hospitality and accommodation in Grenada offer a wide range of options to suit every traveler's preferences and budget, from luxurious resorts to cozy guesthouses and everything in between. As a popular tourist destination, Grenada boasts a vibrant hospitality industry that caters to the needs and expectations of visitors from around the world.

One of the most common types of accommodation in Grenada is the resort, which offers a full range of amenities and services for guests seeking a relaxing and indulgent vacation experience. Many resorts are located along the island's stunning coastline, offering beachfront accommodations with breathtaking views of the Caribbean Sea. These resorts typically feature spacious rooms or suites, multiple dining options, swimming pools, spas, and recreational facilities such as tennis courts, golf courses, and water sports centers.

For travelers seeking a more intimate and authentic experience, guesthouses and bed-and-breakfasts are popular options in Grenada. These smaller establishments are often family-owned and operated, providing personalized service and a warm, welcoming atmosphere. Guesthouses and bed-and-breakfasts are scattered throughout the island, offering cozy rooms, home-cooked meals, and opportunities to connect with local hosts and fellow travelers. Grenada is also home to a growing number of eco-friendly and sustainable accommodations that cater to environmentally conscious travelers. Eco-resorts, eco-lodges, and boutique hotels prioritize sustainability and conservation, offering eco-friendly amenities, locally sourced cuisine, and opportunities for eco-tourism activities such as hiking, birdwatching, and nature walks. These accommodations provide a unique opportunity to experience Grenada's natural beauty while minimizing environmental impact. In addition to traditional accommodations, Grenada also offers unique lodging options such as villas, cottages, and apartments for travelers seeking a home-away-from-home experience. These self-catering accommodations are ideal for families, groups, or long-term visitors who prefer the independence and flexibility of having their own space. Villas and cottages are available in various sizes and locations, ranging from secluded hillside retreats to beachfront properties with private pools and gardens.

No matter where you choose to stay in Grenada, you can expect warm hospitality, friendly service, and a genuine commitment to ensuring a memorable and enjoyable experience for every guest. Whether you're seeking luxury and relaxation or adventure and exploration, Grenada's hospitality industry has something for everyone, making it the perfect destination for your next getaway.

Shopping in Grenada: Souvenirs and Local Crafts

Shopping in Grenada offers a delightful experience for visitors looking to take home a piece of the island's vibrant culture and heritage. From bustling markets to charming boutiques, Grenada boasts a diverse array of shopping opportunities that showcase the island's unique crafts, spices, and souvenirs.

One of the most popular shopping destinations in Grenada is the Grand Anse Craft and Spice Market, located near the famous Grand Anse Beach. Here, visitors can browse stalls filled with a colorful array of handmade crafts, souvenirs, and local products, including pottery, wood carvings, woven baskets, jewelry, and spices. The market is a bustling hub of activity, with vendors eager to share their knowledge of Grenadian culture and traditions with shoppers.

Another must-visit shopping spot in Grenada is the St. George's Market Square, located in the heart of the capital city. This historic market dates back to the 18th century and offers a diverse selection of goods, including fresh produce, spices, clothing, and handicrafts. Visitors can wander through the maze of stalls, sampling local delicacies, bargaining with vendors, and immersing themselves in the vibrant sights, sounds, and smells of the market.

For those seeking high-quality handicrafts and artisanal products, Grenada is home to a number of boutique shops and galleries that showcase the work of local artists and craftsmen. These establishments offer a curated selection of unique and one-of-a-kind items, ranging from handmade clothing and accessories to paintings, sculptures, and ceramics. Shopping at these boutique shops not only supports local artisans but also allows visitors to acquire truly special souvenirs and mementos of their time in Grenada.

Grenada is also famous for its spices, particularly nutmeg, cinnamon, and cloves, which are grown and harvested on the island. Visitors can purchase a variety of spices and spice products at specialty shops and markets throughout Grenada, including ground spices, whole spices, flavored oils, and handmade spice blends. Spice tours are also available, allowing visitors to learn about the cultivation and processing of spices and to purchase fresh, locally sourced products directly from the source.

In addition to crafts and spices, Grenada is known for its chocolate, with several local producers crafting high-quality chocolate bars, truffles, and other confections using locally grown cocoa beans. Visitors can tour cocoa plantations, visit chocolate factories, and sample a variety of chocolate products at specialty shops and chocolatiers across the island.

Overall, shopping in Grenada is an enriching and enjoyable experience, offering visitors the opportunity to discover the island's rich cultural heritage, support local artisans and businesses, and take home a piece of the Spice Isle to treasure for years to come. Whether browsing bustling markets, exploring boutique shops, or sampling local delicacies, shopping in Grenada is sure to delight and inspire visitors of all ages.

Agriculture and Farming: Beyond Nutmeg and Cocoa

Agriculture and farming in Grenada extend far beyond the cultivation of nutmeg and cocoa, encompassing a diverse range of crops and livestock that contribute to the island's economy and food security. While nutmeg and cocoa are indeed significant agricultural exports, Grenada's fertile soil and tropical climate support the cultivation of a variety of other crops, including bananas, citrus fruits, avocados, breadfruit, and root vegetables.

Banana cultivation has a long history in Grenada and remains an important agricultural activity, with bananas being one of the island's top export crops. Smallholder farmers cultivate bananas on steep hillsides and in fertile valleys, utilizing sustainable farming practices to minimize environmental impact and maximize yields. Grenada's bananas are known for their high quality and unique flavor, making them sought after in both domestic and international markets.

Citrus fruits, including oranges, grapefruits, and limes, are also grown in abundance in Grenada, thriving in the island's warm climate and fertile soil. Citrus orchards dot the landscape, producing juicy, flavorful fruits that are used in everything from refreshing juices and desserts to savory dishes and cocktails. Grenada's citrus industry supports local farmers and provides fresh, vitamin-rich produce to both residents and visitors year-round.

Avocado cultivation is on the rise in Grenada, with farmers capitalizing on the growing demand for this nutritious and versatile fruit. Avocado trees flourish in Grenada's subtropical climate, producing creamy, buttery avocados that are prized for their flavor and texture. Avocados are used in a variety of dishes in Grenadian cuisine, from salads and sandwiches to dips and spreads, and are also exported to regional and international markets.

Breadfruit is another staple crop in Grenada, with breadfruit trees lining roadsides and filling orchards across the island. Breadfruit is a versatile and nutritious fruit that can be roasted, fried, boiled, or mashed, providing a staple food source for many Grenadians. Breadfruit trees are also valued for their shade and beauty, with their large, broad leaves providing shelter from the sun and their fragrant flowers attracting pollinators.

Root vegetables such as yams, sweet potatoes, and dasheen are grown in Grenada's fertile soils, providing a source of sustenance for local communities and adding diversity to the island's culinary offerings. These hearty and nutritious crops are cultivated using traditional farming methods, with farmers tending to small plots of land and harvesting crops by hand.

Livestock farming is also practiced in Grenada, with farmers raising cattle, goats, pigs, and poultry for meat, milk, and eggs. Livestock farming is typically small-scale and integrated with other agricultural activities, with animals grazing on pastureland and supplementing their diets with locally grown feed.

Overall, agriculture and farming in Grenada are diverse and dynamic, with farmers harnessing the island's natural resources and traditional knowledge to cultivate a variety of crops and livestock. By embracing sustainable farming practices and promoting agricultural innovation, Grenada continues to strengthen its agricultural sector and enhance food security for its people.

Sustainable Tourism Initiatives: Preserving Paradise for Generations

Sustainable tourism initiatives in Grenada are at the forefront of efforts to preserve the island's natural beauty and cultural heritage for future generations. Recognizing the importance of responsible tourism practices, Grenada has implemented various initiatives and programs aimed at minimizing environmental impact, supporting local communities, and promoting cultural conservation.

One key aspect of sustainable tourism in Grenada is the protection and preservation of the island's marine and coastal ecosystems. Grenada's marine environment is home to diverse coral reefs, seagrass beds, and marine life, making it a popular destination for snorkeling, diving, and marine-based tourism activities. To protect these valuable ecosystems, Grenada has established marine protected areas, such as the Moliniere-Beausejour Marine Protected Area and the Woburn-Clarkes Court Bay Marine Protected Area, where fishing and other activities are regulated to minimize disturbance and promote conservation.

In addition to marine conservation efforts, Grenada is also committed to sustainable land management and biodiversity conservation. The Grand Etang National Park and Forest Reserve, located in the central highlands of Grenada, is a prime example of Grenada's commitment to preserving its natural heritage. The park is home to diverse flora and fauna, including tropical rainforest, crater lakes, and endemic species such as the Grenada dove and the Mona monkey. Visitors to the park can explore hiking trails, birdwatching spots, and scenic viewpoints while learning about the importance of conservation and environmental stewardship.

Community-based tourism initiatives play a vital role in promoting sustainable tourism in Grenada, empowering local communities to benefit from tourism while preserving their cultural traditions and way of life. Community-based tourism projects such as the Belmont Estate and the Laura Herb and Spice Garden offer visitors the opportunity to experience Grenadian culture and heritage firsthand, through guided tours, workshops, and cultural activities. These initiatives not only provide economic opportunities for local residents but also foster a sense of pride and ownership in their cultural heritage.

Grenada's commitment to sustainable tourism extends beyond environmental and cultural conservation to include social and economic sustainability as well. The Grenada Tourism Authority works closely with tourism stakeholders, including hoteliers, tour operators, and local businesses, to promote responsible tourism practices and ensure that tourism benefits are distributed equitably throughout the community. Efforts to promote sustainable tourism in Grenada include initiatives to support small and medium-sized enterprises, enhance tourism infrastructure, and provide training and capacity-building opportunities for local residents.

Overall, sustainable tourism initiatives in Grenada are essential for preserving the island's natural beauty, cultural heritage, and way of life for future generations. By embracing responsible tourism practices and promoting sustainable development, Grenada is ensuring that its paradise remains intact for visitors to enjoy for years to come.

Grenada's Role in the Caribbean Community: Cooperation and Collaboration

Grenada plays a significant role in the Caribbean Community (CARICOM), a regional organization dedicated to promoting economic integration, cooperation, and collaboration among its member states. As one of the smallest countries in CARICOM, Grenada contributes to the organization's objectives through active participation in various initiatives and programs aimed at advancing the interests of the region as a whole.

One of the key areas of cooperation within CARICOM is economic integration, with member states working together to facilitate trade, investment, and economic development across the region. Grenada benefits from CARICOM's Common External Tariff (CET), which promotes intra-regional trade by harmonizing tariffs on goods imported from outside the Caribbean Community. This allows Grenadian businesses to access markets in other CARICOM countries on preferential terms, fostering economic growth and regional integration.

In addition to economic cooperation, CARICOM member states collaborate on a wide range of issues, including climate change, disaster management, and sustainable development. Grenada, like other small island developing states in the Caribbean, is particularly vulnerable to the impacts of climate change, including rising sea levels, extreme weather events, and loss of biodiversity. Through CARICOM, Grenada participates in regional initiatives aimed at addressing these challenges, such as the Caribbean Community Climate Change Centre (CCCCC) and the Caribbean Disaster Emergency Management Agency (CDEMA), which provide technical assistance, capacity building, and financial support to help countries adapt to and mitigate the effects of climate change and natural disasters.

CARICOM also serves as a platform for cooperation on social and cultural issues, with member states collaborating to promote education, health, and cultural exchange programs throughout the region. Grenada participates in various CARICOM-sponsored initiatives aimed at improving access to education and healthcare, enhancing cultural exchange and promoting regional identity and unity.

In the realm of politics and diplomacy, Grenada is an active participant in CARICOM's efforts to promote peace, security, and stability in the Caribbean region and beyond. CARICOM member states work together to address common challenges, such as transnational crime, human trafficking, and drug trafficking, through joint initiatives and cooperation with international partners.

Overall, Grenada's role in CARICOM reflects its commitment to regional cooperation and collaboration, as well as its recognition of the importance of working together with its Caribbean neighbors to address shared challenges and pursue common goals. Through its active participation in CARICOM, Grenada contributes to the collective strength and resilience of the Caribbean Community, ensuring a brighter future for all its members.

Grenada's Influence on the World Stage: Diplomacy and Global Relations

Grenada, though a small island nation, has made significant contributions to the global stage through its diplomacy and engagement in international relations. While its size may not match that of larger nations, Grenada's influence extends far beyond its shores, shaping global discussions on issues ranging from climate change to human rights.

One notable area where Grenada has exerted influence is in the realm of climate change and environmental sustainability. As a small island developing state, Grenada is particularly vulnerable to the impacts of climate change, including rising sea levels, extreme weather events, and loss of biodiversity. In international forums such as the United Nations Climate Change Conferences (COP), Grenada has been a vocal advocate for ambitious climate action and increased support for adaptation and mitigation efforts in vulnerable countries. Grenada's participation in global climate negotiations has helped to raise awareness of the unique challenges faced by small island nations and to mobilize international support for addressing the root causes of climate change.

Grenada has also played a role in promoting peace and security on the world stage through its participation in regional and international peacekeeping efforts. As a member of the Caribbean Community (CARICOM), Grenada has contributed troops to peacekeeping missions under the auspices of the United Nations, including deployments to conflict zones such as Haiti and Liberia. Grenadian peacekeepers have earned praise for their professionalism, dedication, and commitment to upholding peace and stability in troubled regions, reflecting Grenada's commitment to global peace and security.

In addition to its efforts in climate change and peacekeeping, Grenada has also been active in promoting human rights and social justice on the world stage. Grenada has ratified various international human rights treaties and conventions and has worked to uphold human rights principles in its domestic policies and practices. Grenada's engagement in international human rights forums has helped to raise awareness of human rights issues in the Caribbean region and to promote dialogue and cooperation on addressing these challenges at the global level.

Furthermore, Grenada has sought to strengthen its ties with other countries through bilateral and multilateral partnerships, diplomatic exchanges, and cultural diplomacy. Grenadian diplomats work tirelessly to represent the interests of their country abroad, advocating for Grenada's priorities and building relationships with foreign governments, international organizations, and civil society groups. Grenada's diplomatic efforts have helped to enhance its visibility and influence on the world stage, contributing to its status as a respected member of the international community.

Overall, Grenada's influence on the world stage is a testament to its diplomatic prowess, strategic engagement, and commitment to addressing global challenges. Despite its size, Grenada punches above its weight in international affairs, making meaningful contributions to shaping the future of our planet and advancing the cause of peace, justice, and sustainability for all.

Grenada's Literary Heritage: Words that Reflect the Soul

Grenada's literary heritage is a rich tapestry woven with the threads of history, culture, and creativity. Despite its small size, Grenada has produced a remarkable array of writers, poets, and storytellers whose works reflect the soul of the island and its people.

One of the most celebrated figures in Grenadian literature is Derek Walcott, a Nobel Prize-winning poet and playwright who was born in St. Lucia but spent much of his life in Grenada. Walcott's poetry is deeply influenced by the Caribbean landscape, culture, and history, exploring themes of identity, colonialism, and the search for belonging. His masterpiece, "Omeros," is an epic poem that draws inspiration from Homer's "Odyssey" while capturing the essence of life in the Caribbean.

Another prominent Grenadian writer is Merle Collins, whose novels and short stories offer vivid portrayals of Grenadian life and society. Collins' work often explores themes of race, gender, and social justice, shedding light on the complexities of post-colonial identity and the struggles of ordinary people in a changing world. Her novel "Angel" is a powerful coming-of-age story set against the backdrop of Grenada's turbulent history.

Grenada has also produced a number of poets whose lyrical verse captures the beauty and rhythm of the island. Olive Senior, a Jamaican-born poet of Grenadian descent, is known for her evocative poetry that explores themes of memory, identity, and belonging. Her collection "Gardening in the Tropics" is a homage to the Caribbean landscape and the people who inhabit it, celebrating the resilience and spirit of the region.

In addition to poetry and prose, Grenada has a vibrant oral storytelling tradition, passed down through generations by griots, or oral historians. These storytellers weave tales of folklore, mythology, and everyday life, preserving Grenada's cultural heritage and transmitting it to future generations. Through their stories, Grenadians connect with their past, celebrate their present, and envision their future.

Grenada's literary heritage is a testament to the power of words to shape our understanding of the world and ourselves. From the epic poetry of Derek Walcott to the poignant prose of Merle Collins to the timeless tales of oral tradition, Grenadian writers have left an indelible mark on the literary landscape, enriching our lives with their words and reflecting the soul of their island home.

Sports and Recreation: Thrills on Land and Sea

Sports and recreation in Grenada encompass a wide range of activities that showcase the island's natural beauty and adventurous spirit. From land-based sports to water-based pursuits, Grenadians and visitors alike have plenty of options for staying active and enjoying the great outdoors.

Cricket holds a special place in Grenadian culture and is considered the national sport. The sport has a long and storied history on the island, with cricket matches being a common sight in local communities and schools. Grenada has produced several notable cricketers who have represented the West Indies in international competitions, including Sir Everton Weekes, who is regarded as one of the greatest batsmen of all time.

Football, or soccer as it's known in the United States, is also popular in Grenada, with numerous teams and leagues competing at both the amateur and professional levels. The Grenada national football team competes in regional and international competitions, showcasing the talent and passion for the sport that exists on the island. Football matches are a lively and exciting affair, with fans cheering on their favorite teams with gusto.

Basketball has a growing following in Grenada, particularly among young people, with courts and facilities available in communities across the island. The Grenada Basketball Association organizes leagues and tournaments for players of all ages and skill levels, providing opportunities for competition and camaraderie. Basketball games are a vibrant and energetic affair, with players displaying skill and athleticism on the court.

In addition to traditional sports, Grenada offers a variety of recreational activities for those who prefer to explore the outdoors. Hiking is a popular pastime, with numerous trails winding through Grenada's lush rainforests, rugged mountains, and coastal landscapes. The Concord Falls Trail, Mt. Qua Qua Trail, and Seven Sisters Waterfalls Trail are just a few examples of the scenic hikes that await adventurers in Grenada.

Water sports enthusiasts will find no shortage of thrills in Grenada's crystal-clear waters. Snorkeling and diving are favorite activities, with vibrant coral reefs, underwater caves, and shipwrecks to explore. The Moliniere Underwater Sculpture Park, created by British sculptor Jason deCaires Taylor, is a unique underwater gallery where visitors can admire sculptures submerged beneath the sea.

Sailing and yachting are also popular pastimes in Grenada, with the island's sheltered bays and steady trade winds providing ideal conditions for cruising and racing. The annual Grenada Sailing Week attracts sailors from around the world, who come to compete in a series of regattas and enjoy the island's hospitality and natural beauty.

Whether on land or at sea, sports and recreation in Grenada offer endless opportunities for adventure, relaxation, and fun. With its stunning landscapes, warm climate, and friendly people, Grenada is truly a paradise for outdoor enthusiasts of all ages and interests.

Exploring Grenada's Nightlife: From Calypso to Rum Punch

Exploring Grenada's nightlife is like stepping into a vibrant tapestry woven with rhythms, flavors, and experiences that captivate the senses. As the sun sets over the island, a new energy emerges, inviting locals and visitors alike to immerse themselves in the pulsating beat of Grenadian culture.

Music is at the heart of Grenada's nightlife scene, with the infectious rhythms of calypso, soca, and reggae setting the tone for evenings filled with dancing and revelry. Whether you're strolling along the streets of St. George's or venturing into one of the island's many nightclubs and bars, you're sure to encounter live music that gets your feet tapping and hips swaying.

Calypso, with its catchy melodies and witty lyrics, is a beloved genre in Grenada, reflecting the island's colorful history and cultural traditions. Local calypsonians, known as "calypsonians," perform at venues across the island, entertaining audiences with their storytelling prowess and lively stage presence. During the annual Grenada Carnival, calypso competitions take center stage, showcasing the talent and creativity of Grenada's musical community.

Soca music, with its high-energy beats and infectious melodies, is another staple of Grenada's nightlife scene, especially during the Carnival season. Soca parties and fetes, known for their lively atmosphere and extravagant costumes, are a highlight of the Carnival calendar, drawing revelers from near and far to celebrate life and music in true Grenadian style.

Of course, no night out in Grenada would be complete without sampling the island's signature libation: rum punch. Made with locally-produced rum, fresh fruit juices, and a hint of spice, rum punch is the perfect companion for a night of dancing and socializing. Whether you're sipping cocktails at a beachside bar or enjoying a homemade concoction at a local rum shop, you'll find that rum punch is as much a part of Grenada's nightlife as the music itself.

In addition to music and drinks, Grenada's nightlife also offers a variety of dining options to suit every palate. From street food vendors serving up savory snacks like fried plantains and roti to upscale restaurants specializing in gourmet cuisine, there's no shortage of delicious fare to satisfy your hunger after a night of dancing and fun.

As the night unfolds, you may find yourself drawn to one of Grenada's many cultural events and festivals, where you can immerse yourself in the traditions and customs of the island. From art exhibitions and theater performances to street parties and cultural shows, there's always something exciting happening after dark in Grenada.

Whether you're looking for a lively dance floor or a quiet corner to enjoy a drink and soak in the atmosphere, Grenada's nightlife has something for everyone. With its rich musical heritage, delicious cuisine, and warm hospitality, Grenada offers an unforgettable nightlife experience that will leave you wanting more.

Grenada's Healthcare System: Providing Care for All

Grenada's healthcare system is built on a foundation of accessibility, quality, and inclusivity, striving to ensure that all residents have access to essential healthcare services. As a small island nation in the Caribbean, Grenada faces unique challenges in delivering healthcare to its population, but it has made significant strides in improving health outcomes and expanding access to care.

The government of Grenada oversees the country's healthcare system, which is primarily funded through taxation and supplemented by contributions from the National Insurance Scheme (NIS). The Ministry of Health is responsible for setting healthcare policies, regulating healthcare providers, and overseeing the delivery of services across the island.

Primary healthcare services are provided through a network of health centers and clinics located in communities throughout Grenada. These facilities offer a range of services, including preventive care, immunizations, maternal and child health services, and treatment for common illnesses and injuries. Access to primary care is essential for promoting wellness and preventing more serious health problems, and the government of Grenada has invested in expanding and improving primary care services to reach more people across the island.

In addition to primary care, Grenada's healthcare system includes secondary and tertiary care facilities that provide more specialized medical services. The General Hospital in St. George's is the largest hospital in Grenada and serves as the main referral center for the island. It offers a wide range of medical and surgical services, including emergency care, obstetrics and gynecology, pediatrics, and internal medicine. The hospital also has specialized departments for cardiology, oncology, orthopedics, and other areas of medicine.

Grenada's healthcare system also includes private healthcare providers, including doctors, dentists, and specialists, who offer services outside of the public sector. Many Grenadians choose to access healthcare through private providers for reasons such as convenience, shorter wait times, or access to specialized services not available in the public sector. Private healthcare in Grenada is regulated by the government to ensure quality and safety standards are met.

Despite progress in improving healthcare services, Grenada still faces challenges in areas such as access to care in remote areas, availability of specialized services, and workforce shortages. The government continues to invest in infrastructure, technology, and human resources to address these challenges and improve health outcomes for all Grenadians.

Overall, Grenada's healthcare system is committed to providing quality care for all residents, regardless of their ability to pay. With a focus on preventive care, accessibility, and quality improvement, Grenada is working towards achieving better health outcomes and a higher standard of living for its population.

Disaster Preparedness and Resilience: Weathering the Storms

Disaster preparedness and resilience are crucial aspects of life in Grenada, a small island nation located in the hurricane-prone Caribbean region. With its lush landscapes, pristine beaches, and vibrant culture, Grenada is a paradise for residents and visitors alike. However, the island's geographical location also exposes it to natural hazards, including hurricanes, tropical storms, earthquakes, and landslides.

The government of Grenada recognizes the importance of proactive measures to mitigate the impact of disasters and protect the safety and well-being of its citizens. Grenada's National Disaster Management Agency (NaDMA) is responsible for coordinating disaster preparedness, response, and recovery efforts across the country. NaDMA works closely with other government agencies, non-governmental organizations, and international partners to develop and implement comprehensive disaster management plans and strategies. One of the key components of Grenada's disaster preparedness efforts is public education and awareness. NaDMA conducts outreach programs and campaigns to educate residents about the risks posed by natural hazards and the steps they can take to protect themselves and their families. This includes providing information on evacuation routes, emergency shelters, and disaster supplies, as well as tips for securing property and belongings before a storm. Grenada has also invested in building resilient infrastructure to withstand the impact of natural disasters. This includes constructing hurricane-resistant buildings, retrofitting critical facilities such as hospitals and schools, and implementing flood mitigation measures in vulnerable areas. The government has also developed building codes and standards to ensure that new construction projects adhere to strict safety guidelines. In addition to physical infrastructure, Grenada has established early warning systems to alert residents to impending natural disasters. The Caribbean Disaster Emergency Management Agency (CDEMA) operates a regional early warning system that provides timely information about hurricanes, tropical storms, earthquakes, and other hazards. Grenada's Emergency Operations Center (EOC) coordinates the dissemination of warnings and instructions to the public, helping to ensure that residents are prepared and able to take appropriate action.

Despite these efforts, Grenada remains vulnerable to the impact of natural disasters, and ongoing challenges such as climate change and limited resources pose ongoing threats to the island's resilience. However, through proactive planning, investment in infrastructure, and community engagement, Grenada is working to build a more resilient society capable of weathering the storms that may come its way.

Social Issues and Challenges: Building a Stronger Community

In Grenada, like in many places around the world, there are social issues and challenges that the community faces as it strives to build a stronger, more cohesive society. While Grenada is known for its natural beauty and warm hospitality, it is not immune to the complexities of modern life and the social issues that accompany them.

One of the key social issues facing Grenada is poverty. While the country has made progress in reducing poverty rates over the years, there are still significant disparities in income and wealth distribution. Many Grenadians struggle to make ends meet, particularly in rural areas where economic opportunities may be limited. Addressing poverty requires not only economic growth but also targeted social programs and policies to support vulnerable populations and ensure that everyone has access to basic necessities such as food, shelter, and healthcare.

Education is another area of concern in Grenada. While the country has made strides in improving access to education, particularly at the primary and secondary levels, there are still challenges related to quality and equity. Limited resources, overcrowded classrooms, and a shortage of

103

qualified teachers can hinder educational outcomes for students, particularly those from disadvantaged backgrounds. Addressing these challenges requires investment in education infrastructure, teacher training, and curriculum development to ensure that all students have access to a high-quality education that prepares them for success in the future.

Healthcare is another social issue that Grenada grapples with. While the country has made progress in improving access to healthcare services, there are still disparities in access and quality of care, particularly in rural and remote areas. Limited healthcare infrastructure, shortages of medical supplies and equipment, and a shortage of healthcare workers can all contribute to challenges in delivering healthcare services to all Grenadians. Addressing these issues requires investment in healthcare infrastructure, training and retaining healthcare professionals, and implementing policies to improve access to care for all residents.

Crime and violence are also social issues that Grenada faces. While the country has relatively low crime rates compared to other countries in the region, there are still concerns about crime, particularly in urban areas. Drug trafficking, gang activity, and interpersonal violence can all contribute to feelings of insecurity and instability in communities. Addressing these issues requires a multi-faceted approach that includes law enforcement, community engagement, and addressing underlying social and economic factors that contribute to crime and violence.

Finally, social issues related to gender equality and social inclusion are also important considerations in Grenada. While the country has made progress in advancing gender equality and protecting the rights of marginalized groups, there are still challenges related to gender-based violence, discrimination, and unequal access to opportunities. Addressing these issues requires concerted efforts to promote gender equality, protect the rights of marginalized groups, and ensure that everyone has equal access to opportunities and resources.

Overall, addressing social issues and challenges in Grenada requires a comprehensive approach that involves government action, community engagement, and collaboration between various stakeholders. By working together to address these issues, Grenada can build a stronger, more inclusive society where everyone has the opportunity to thrive.

Volunteerism and Philanthropy: Giving Back to Grenada

Volunteerism and philanthropy play vital roles in Grenada's community fabric, embodying the spirit of giving back and fostering social cohesion. Across the island, individuals, organizations, and businesses are engaged in various initiatives aimed at improving the lives of others and building a stronger, more resilient society.

One avenue through which volunteerism thrives in Grenada is through community-based organizations and non-profit groups. These organizations address a wide range of issues, from education and healthcare to environmental conservation and social welfare. Volunteers donate their time, skills, and resources to support these initiatives, whether it's tutoring children, organizing clean-up campaigns, or providing assistance to vulnerable populations.

International volunteer programs also contribute significantly to Grenada's volunteerism landscape. Many volunteers from around the world choose to spend time in Grenada working on community development projects, environmental conservation efforts, or disaster relief initiatives. These volunteers bring diverse perspectives and expertise to local challenges, helping to catalyze positive change and build capacity within Grenada's communities.

Philanthropy, both individual and corporate, is another important aspect of giving back in Grenada. Many individuals and families in Grenada are actively involved in philanthropic endeavors, donating money, resources, and time to support causes they care about. From funding scholarships for students to supporting healthcare facilities and social service organizations, philanthropy plays a crucial role in addressing pressing needs and promoting social welfare in Grenada.

Corporate philanthropy is also on the rise in Grenada, with businesses and companies stepping up to support community initiatives and social causes. Through corporate social responsibility programs, businesses contribute to projects and programs that benefit local communities, whether it's investing in education and youth development, supporting environmental conservation efforts, or providing disaster relief assistance.

In addition to volunteering and philanthropy, Grenada's diaspora community plays a significant role in giving back to the island. Many Grenadians who live abroad maintain strong ties to their homeland and contribute to its development through remittances, charitable donations, and involvement in community projects. The support of the diaspora community is instrumental in addressing challenges and fostering progress in Grenada.

Overall, volunteerism and philanthropy are integral parts of Grenada's social fabric, reflecting the collective commitment of its people to make a positive impact and create a brighter future for all. Through acts of kindness, generosity, and solidarity, individuals and organizations in Grenada are working together to build a stronger, more resilient, and more compassionate society for generations to come.

Exploring Grenada's Neighborhood: Relations with Nearby Islands

Exploring Grenada's neighborhood reveals a dynamic network of relations with nearby islands, reflecting a rich tapestry of historical, cultural, and economic connections. Situated in the southeastern Caribbean Sea, Grenada is part of the Lesser Antilles archipelago, surrounded by a cluster of islands, each with its own unique identity and character.

To the north of Grenada lies the island of St. Vincent, with which Grenada shares close historical ties. Both islands were once part of the British Windward Islands colony and have a shared colonial history. Today, Grenada and St. Vincent maintain diplomatic relations and collaborate on regional initiatives through organizations such as the Organization of Eastern Caribbean States (OECS).

To the south of Grenada lies the island of Trinidad, the largest and most populous island in the southern Caribbean. Grenada's relationship with Trinidad is characterized by economic interdependence, with trade and commerce playing a significant role in bilateral relations. Trinidad is a major trading partner for Grenada, particularly in the areas of energy, manufacturing, and agriculture.

To the west of Grenada lies the island of Carriacou, which is part of Grenada's territory along with the smaller island of Petite Martinique. Carriacou shares strong cultural and familial ties with Grenada, and residents of both islands often travel back and forth for work, education, and social events. The relationship between Grenada and Carriacou is characterized by mutual support and cooperation, with Grenada providing essential services and infrastructure support to its sister island.

To the east of Grenada lies the island of Barbados, which shares historical connections with Grenada dating back to the colonial era. Both islands were once part of the British Empire and have since gained independence, forging their own paths while maintaining friendly relations. Barbados is a popular destination for Grenadians, who travel there for tourism, education, and business opportunities.

In addition to these neighboring islands, Grenada also maintains relations with other Caribbean nations and participates in regional organizations such as the Caribbean Community (CARICOM) and the Association of Caribbean States (ACS). These relationships are crucial for Grenada's development and security, as they provide opportunities for cooperation, collaboration, and mutual support in areas such as trade, tourism, and disaster management.

Overall, Grenada's neighborhood is characterized by a diverse array of relationships with nearby islands, each contributing to the island's rich tapestry of culture, history, and identity. Through diplomacy, trade, and cultural exchange, Grenada continues to strengthen its bonds with its neighbors, forging a brighter future for the entire Caribbean region.

Grenada's Future: Opportunities and Challenges Ahead

Grenada stands at a pivotal moment in its history, poised on the threshold of a future filled with both opportunities and challenges. As the island nation navigates the complexities of the 21st century, it must confront a range of economic, social, and environmental factors that will shape its trajectory in the years to come.

One of the key opportunities for Grenada lies in its burgeoning tourism industry. With its stunning natural landscapes, pristine beaches, and vibrant culture, Grenada has the potential to become a premier destination for travelers seeking authentic Caribbean experiences. The government has been actively promoting tourism development through investment in infrastructure, marketing campaigns, and sustainable tourism initiatives, aiming to capitalize on the island's unique attractions and boost economic growth.

Furthermore, Grenada's strategic location in the Caribbean region presents opportunities for trade and commerce. The island's proximity to major markets in North America, South America, and Europe positions it as a potential hub for international trade and investment. By leveraging its geographic advantage and fostering a business-friendly environment, Grenada can attract foreign investment, stimulate economic activity, and create job opportunities for its citizens.

In addition to tourism and trade, Grenada has opportunities for growth in sectors such as agriculture, renewable energy, and education. The island's fertile soil and favorable climate make it well-suited for agricultural production, particularly in areas such as nutmeg, cocoa, and spices. By investing in agricultural innovation and value-added processing, Grenada can enhance its agricultural productivity, increase exports, and improve food security for its population.

Moreover, Grenada has vast potential in renewable energy development, with abundant sunlight and wind resources that can be harnessed to reduce dependency on fossil fuels and mitigate climate change. The government has already taken steps to promote renewable energy initiatives, including the implementation of solar power projects and the exploration of geothermal energy resources, signaling a commitment to sustainability and environmental stewardship.

Despite these opportunities, Grenada also faces a set of challenges that must be addressed to ensure a prosperous future. Economic diversification is a pressing issue, as the island's reliance on tourism and agriculture leaves it vulnerable to external shocks and fluctuations in global markets. To build a more resilient economy, Grenada must invest in sectors such as technology, innovation, and entrepreneurship, fostering a culture of creativity and innovation that drives sustainable growth.

Furthermore, Grenada must address social issues such as poverty, inequality, and access to healthcare and education. While the government has made strides in improving social services and infrastructure, there is still work to be done to ensure that all Grenadians have access to quality healthcare, education, and opportunities for upward mobility. By investing in human capital and social development, Grenada can empower its citizens and build a more inclusive society.

Environmental sustainability is another critical challenge facing Grenada, as the island grapples with issues such as climate change, deforestation, and marine pollution. The government has implemented measures to protect the environment, including the establishment of marine protected areas and the promotion of sustainable land management practices. However, concerted efforts are needed to address these challenges and safeguard

Grenada's natural resources for future generations.

In conclusion, Grenada's future is filled with promise, yet it also presents significant challenges that must be overcome. By capitalizing on its strengths, addressing its weaknesses, and fostering collaboration and innovation, Grenada can chart a course toward a brighter, more sustainable future for all its citizens.

Epilogue

As we conclude our journey through the vibrant tapestry of Grenada, we are left with a profound appreciation for the beauty, resilience, and spirit of this enchanting island nation. From its lush rainforests and pristine beaches to its rich cultural heritage and warm hospitality, Grenada captivates the imagination and leaves an indelible mark on all who visit.

Throughout this exploration, we have delved into Grenada's fascinating history, from its indigenous peoples and colonial past to its journey to independence and its role on the world stage. We have marveled at the island's natural wonders, from its cascading waterfalls and verdant valleys to its colorful coral reefs and diverse marine life.

We have savored the flavors of Grenada's cuisine, with its tantalizing blend of spices, fresh seafood, and tropical fruits. We have danced to the rhythm of Grenada's music, from the pulsating beat of calypso and soca to the soul-stirring melodies of steelpan and reggae.

We have explored Grenada's bustling markets, where vendors sell everything from handmade crafts and souvenirs to locally grown produce and spices. We have wandered through

Grenada's historic towns and villages, where colonial architecture blends seamlessly with Caribbean charm.

We have witnessed Grenada's commitment to sustainability and environmental stewardship, from its efforts to protect its natural habitats and wildlife to its initiatives to promote renewable energy and sustainable tourism.

As we bid farewell to Grenada, we are reminded of the importance of preserving and cherishing this precious gem of the Caribbean. Whether as a tourist, a resident, or an admirer from afar, Grenada will always hold a special place in our hearts, inspiring us with its beauty, enriching us with its culture, and reminding us of the importance of living in harmony with nature and each other. Grenada's story is far from over; it is a story of resilience, determination, and hope, and it will continue to unfold for generations to come.

Made in the USA
Coppell, TX
19 March 2025

47250816R10066